THE ULTIMATE
NEW YORK JETS
NFL TRIVIA GUIDE

400 AMAZING QUIZZES

AND FUN FACTS TO TEST YOUR WIT!

TYLER CRAWFORD

ISBN: 9798531303653

INTRODUCTION

The New York Jets football franchise was founded 62 years ago on August 14, 1959. The team was originally called the New York Titans and the first stadium they played at was the Polo Grounds. Four years later, the New York Titans became the New York Jets since their stadium was very close to Laguardia airport. The Jets played at their new field (Shea Stadium) for twenty years. In 1984, the team moved to a new stadium called the Meadowlands in New Jersey. The Jets remained at the Meadowlands for sixteen years. In 2010, the team moved to a brand new stadium nearby called Met Life Stadium.

As a young teenager, I became a fan of the New York Jets and have been a loyal fan for a few decades. I recall the many Sundays I attended games at Shea Stadium, the Meadowlands and Met Life Stadium only to see my team suffer many defeats. Despite their rollercoaster and disappointing history, I continue to have hope. The annual

NFL draft and free agency each year is significant since it helps improve the team and build their roster.

As a loyal fan, I attended practices the Jets held at Hofstra University in Uniondale, New York. The New York Jets practiced at that facility for 34 years. In 2008, the Jets acquired Brett Favre in free agency. Once Brett Favre was signed to the club, the practices he attended brought in over 7,000 fans to the team facility. Unfortunately, Brett Favre only played for the Jets for one season. In 2008, the New York Jets organization transferred their practice facility to a new modern 26 acre complex in Florham Park, New Jersey. This new practice field holds five 100 yard playing fields with an indoor field house. This new complex has 103-foot high ceilings in its field house and allows the team to have kicking practices there.

Sadly, in 2020, the New York Jets suffered one of the worst seasons in team history with a total record of 2 wins and 14 losses. After the final game of the 2020 season, head coach Adam Gase was fired. In February 2021, defensive coordinator Robert Saleh of the San Francisco 49ers was hired as the new head coach of the Jets. Robert has worked with four other NFL football teams and served in a defense capacity with those clubs.

The NFL draft held from April 29-May 1, 2021 helped acquire several new offensive and defensive players to the team's roster. The New York Jets selected Zach Wilson from Brigham Young University with the second pick of the first round of the draft. GM Joe Douglas addressed the offensive line with their second first round pick by selecting Alijah Vera Tucker. In addition, Joe continued to bolster the offense by selecting wide receiver Elijah Moore in the second round and choosing running back Michael Carter in the fourth round. Hopefully these four draft choices will help ignite their anemic offense.

After several years of being a devoted fan and after conducting much intensive research, I have decided to write The Ultimate New York Jets NFL Trivia Guide. This comprehensive guide covers all aspects of the New York Jets organization from its inception to the present day. This guide covers football trivia on both offensive and defensive sides of the game. In addition, it covers important questions and answers on several of the coaches hired throughout the history of the franchise. I hope you enjoy this guide as much as I did creating it!

Tyler Crawford

TABLE OF CONTENTS

CHAPTER I:
NEW YORK JETS GENERAL TRIVIA
EXAM TIME

1. True or False   The New York Jets were originally called the New York Flyers.

a. True

b. False

2. True or False   Joe Namath led the New York Jets to victory in Super Bowl VI.

A. True

b. False

3. Which position did Pat Leahy play for the New York Jets?

a. Quarterback

b. Running back

c. Place kicker

d. Tight End

4. Which New York Jet player had the most sacks in his career for the team?

a. Shaun Ellis

b. Mark Gastineau

c. John Abraham

d. Joe Klecko

5. Which New York Jets player had the most receiving yards for the team in NFL history?

a. Wayne Chrebet

b. Al Toon

c. Wesley Walker

d. Don Maynard

6. Which New York Jets Kicker attempted 8 field goals in a game with the team?

a. Nick Folk

b. Pat Leahy

c. Jim Turner

d. John Hall

7. Which New York Jets Quarterback fumbled the most times in a game in team history?

a. Chad Pennington

b. Mark Sanchez

c. Richard Todd

d. Ken O'Brien

8. Which two New York Jets Quarterbacks share the franchise record for most completed passes in a game?

a. Mark Sanchez and Brett Favre

b. Joe Namath and Brett Favre

c. Richard Todd and Vinny Testaverde

d. Geno Smith and Ken O"Brien

9. Which New York Jets Quarterback holds the record for being sacked the most times in a game?

a. Mark Sanchez

b. David Norme

c. Ken O'Brien

d. Brett Favre

10. Which New York Jets Quarterback holds the record for the most passes attempted in a game?

a. Brett Favre

b. Joe Namath

c. Ken O"Brien

d. Vinny Testaverde

11. Which New York Jets player is the leading point scorer for the team in franchise history?

a. Pat Leahy

b. Don Maynard

c. Wayne Chrebet

d. Wesley Walker

12. Which player on the New York Jets played the most years with the team?

a. Freeman McNeil

b. Joe Klecko

c. Emerson Boozer

d. Pat Leahy

13. Which New York Jets player had the longest punt return in team history?

a. Andre Roberts

b. Leon Washington

c. Terance Mathis

d. Justin Miller

14. Which New York Jets player had the longest play in team history?

a. Andre Roberts

b. Brad Smith

c. Freeman McNeil

d. Wesley Walker

15. Which New York Jets punter had the longest punt in NFL history?

a. Dave Jennings

b. Steve O'Neal

c. Louie Aguilar

d. Chuck Ramsey

16. True or False   In the 1970's, the New York Jets had two winning seasons.

a. True

b. False

17. Who was the first New York Jet to be inducted into the Pro Football Hall of Fame?

a. Weeb Ewbank

b. Joe Namath

c. Mark Gastineau

d. Don Maynard

18. True or False   In 1969, Pat Leahy kicked three field goals for the New York Jets in the Super Bowl win against the Colts.

a. True

b. False

19. True or False   Don Maynard was the first receiver to reach 10,000 yards in New York Jets history.

a. True

b. False

20. Who was the first New York Jets player to throw for 4,000 yards in a season?

a. Vinny Testaverde

b. Neil O"Donnell

C. Joe Namath

D. Ray Lucas

21. In 1983, the New York Jets selected which Quarterback ahead of Dan Marino?

a. Ken O'Brien

b. Chad Pennington

c. Kellen Clemens

d. Sandy Stephens

22. In what year was the New York Jets founded?

a. 1958

b. 1959

c. 1962

d. 1965

23. In their first game at Shea Stadium, the New York Jets defeated which team by a score of 37- 0?

a. Oakland Raiders

b. Pittsburgh Steelers

c. Cleveland Browns

d. Denver Broncos

24. Which team did the New York Jets defeat to win their only AFC Championship Game?

a. Oakland Raiders

b. Cleveland Browns

c. Baltimore Colts

d. Pittsburgh Steelers

25. Which team did the New York Jets lose to in the "Heidi" game?

a. Baltimore Colts

b. Kansas City Chiefs

c. Oakland Raiders

d. Miami Dolphins

26. Who was the first running back in New York Jets history to rush for over 1,000 yards in a season?

a. Emerson Boozer

b. John Riggins

c. Freeman McNeil

d. Curtis Martin

27. Who was the coach of the New York Jets in 1976?

a. Lou Holtz

b. Walt Michaels

c. Charley Winner

d. Weeb Ewbank

28. Which college did Joe Namath attend?

a. USC

b. UCLA

c. Alabama

d. Pittsburgh

29. What college did Wesley Walker attend?

a. Texas Tech

b. Oregon

c. Oklahoma

d. Nebraska

30. Before coming to the New York Jets, which team did Curtis Martin play for?

a. Miami Dolphins

b. New England Patriots

c. Oakland Raiders

d. Denver Broncos

ANSWERS

1. False   2. False   3. C   4. B   5. D   6. C   7. A   8. C   9. B   10. D

11. A   12. D   13. C   14. B   15. B   16. False   17. A   18. False   19. True   20. C 21. A   22. B   23. D   24. A   25. C   26. B   27. A   28. C   29. A   30. B

CHAPTER II:
NEW YORK JETS PLAYOFFS TRIVIA
EXAM TIME

31. Who was the main running back for the New York Jets in the 1968 playoffs?

a. John Riggins

b. Leon Washington

c. Matt Snell

d. Johnny Hector

32. Who was the opposing Quarterback against the New York Jets in the 1968 Championship game?

a. Daryle Lamonica

b. Ken Stabler

c. Cotton Davison

d. George Blanda

33. Which receiver for the New York Jets had the most receiving yards in the 1968 AFC Championship game?

a. George Sauer

b. Pete Lammons

c. Wesley Walker

d. Don Maynard

34. Who was the Tight End for the New York Jets in the 1968 playoffs?

a. Mark Smolinski

b. Pete Lammons

c. Mickey Shuler

d. Dustin Keller

35. True or False New York Jets players Verlon Biggs and Paul Rochester were tied with one sack apiece in the 1968 AFC Championship game?

a. True

b. False

36. True or False The New York Jets had one interception in the 1968 AFC Championship game.

a. True

b. False

37. Who was the punter for the New York Jets in the 1968 playoffs?

a. Curley Johnson

b. Jim Turner

c. Nick Fold

d. Louie Aguilar

38. How many interceptions did the New York Jets Quarterback throw in the 1968 AFC Championship game?

a. 4

b. 3

c. 2

d. 1

39. How many field goals did the New York Jets placekicker kick in the 1968 AFC Championship game?

a. 1

b. 2

c. 3

d. 4

40. True or False   Joe Namath of the New York Jets had one fumble in the 1968 AFC Championship game?

a. True

b. False

41. Who was the Center for the New York Jets in the 1968 AFC Championship game?

a. John Schmitt

b. Joe Fields

c. Nick Mangold

d. Kevin Mawae

42. Who were the starting cornerbacks for the New York Jets in the 1968 AFC Championship game?

a. Ty Law and Burgess Owens

b. Ken Schroy and Erik McMillan

c. Dainard Paulson and Darryl Ray

d. Johnny Sample and Randy Beverly

43. Who was one of the starting Safeties for the New York Jets in the 1968 AFC Championship game?

a. Burgess Owens

b. Jim Hudson

c. Darryl Ray

d. Bradley McDougald

44. Who were the starting Offensive Tackles for the New York Jets in the 1968 playoffs?

a. Adrian Jones and Marko Cavka

b. Kareem McKenzie

c. Randy Rasmussen and Winston Hill

d. Eric Bateman and Melvin Hayes

45. Who were the starting kickoff returners for the New York Jets in the 1968 playoffs?

a. Bruce Harper and Lou Piccone

b. Aaron Glenn and Dwight Stone

c. Earl Christy and Bake Turner

d. Roscoe Ward and Mike Battle

46. What is the New York Jets all - time playoff record?

a. 13 wins and 12 losses

b. 12 wins and 13 losses

c. 10 wins and 15 losses

d. 11 wins and 14 losses

47. Which team did the New York Jets play in the 1985 Wild Card game?

a. Miami Dolphins

b. Oakland Raiders

c. Cleveland Browns

d. New England Patriots

48. Who was the starting Quarterback for the New York Jets in the 1985 Wild Card game?

a. Ken O'Brien

b. Richard Todd

c. Matt Robinson

d. Pat Ryan

49. What was the total passing yards for the New York Jets Quarterback in the 1985 Wild Card game?

a. 150 yards

b. 200 yards

c. 233 yards

d. 275 yards

50. How many interceptions did the New York Jets Quarterback throw in the 1985 Wild Card game?

a. 2

b. 1

c. 0

d. 3

51. Who was the starting running back for the New York Jets in the 1985 Wild Card game?

a. Johnny Hector

b. Freeman McNeil

c. Shonn Greene

d. Roger Vick

52. Who were the starting receivers for the New York Jets in the 1985 Wild Card game?

a. Johnny Lam Jones and Brandon Marshall

b. Terance Mathis and David Knight

c. Derrick Gaffney and Mickey Shuler

d. Al Toon and Wesley Walker

53. How many times were the New York Jets in the playoffs in team history?

a. 10

b. 12

c. 14

d. 16

54. In the year 2010, the New York Jets lost to which team in the AFC Championship game?

a. Pittsburgh Steelers

b. New England Patriots

c. Buffalo Bills

d. Oakland Raiders

55. In the year 2009, the New York Jets lost to which team in the AFC Championship game?

a. Pittsburgh Steelers

b. Indianapolis Colts

c. New England Patriots

d. Buffalo Bills

56. In 2001, the New York Jets lost to which team in the Wild Card round?

a. Oakland Raiders

b. New England Patriots

c. Pittsburgh Steelers

d. Denver Broncos

57. In 1998, which team did the New York Jets defeat in the Divisional Round?

a. New England Patriots

b. Pittsburgh Steelers

c. Jacksonville Jaguars

d. Kansas City Chiefs

58. In 1998, which team did the New York Jets lose to in the AFC Championship game?

a. New England Patriots

b. Pittsburgh Steelers

c. Buffalo Bills

d. Denver Broncos

59. In 1991, the New York Jets lost to which team in the Wild Card round?

a. New England Patriots

b. Houston Oilers

c. Pittsburgh Steelers

d. Buffalo Bills

60. In 1982, which team did the New York Jets defeat in the Wild Card round of the playoffs?

a. Kansas City Chiefs

b. New England Patriots

c. Cincinnati Bengals

d. Pittsburgh Steelers

61. In 1982, which team did the New York Jets defeat in the Divisional Round of the playoffs?

a. Los Angeles Raiders

b. New England Patriots

c. Denver Broncos

d. Pittsburgh Steelers

62. In 1982, which team did the New York Jets lose to in the AFC Championship game?

a. Pittsburgh Steelers

b. New England Patriots

c. Miami Dolphins

d. Los Angeles Raiders

63. In 2004, which team did the New York Jets defeat in the Wild Card Round of the playoffs?

a. New England Patriots

b. San Diego Chargers

c. Buffalo Bills

d. Kansas City Chiefs

64. In 2004, which team did the New York Jets lose to in the Divisional Round of the playoffs?

a. Denver Broncos

b. New England Patriots

c. Miami Dolphins

d. Pittsburgh Steelers

65. In 2006, which team did the New York Jets lose to in the Wild Card round of the playoffs?

a. Denver Broncos

b. New England Patriots

c. Pittsburgh Steelers

d. Kansas City Chiefs

66. Who were the leading receivers for the New York Jets in the 2010 playoffs?

a. Brandon Marshall and Eric Decker

b. Dedrick Ward and Dwight Stone

c. Santonio Holmes and Braylon Edwards

d. Lavernues Coles and Desmond Kitchings

67. Who was the Quarterback for the New York Jets in the 1998 playoffs?

a. Vinny Testaverde

b. Frank Reich

c. Ray Lucas

d. Chad Pennington

68. Who was the starting running back for the New York Jets in the 2010 playoffs?

a. Curtis Martin

b. Thomas Jones

c. Chris Ivory

d. LaDainian Tomlinson

69. True or False   Joe Namath threw two touchdown passes in the Super Bowl win against the Baltimore Colts.

a. True

b. False

70. Who was the head coach for the New York Jets in the 2004 playoffs?

a. Walt Michaels

b. Bruce Coslet

c. Herm Edwards

d. Eric Mangini

ANSWERS

31. C   32. A   33. D   34. B   35. True   36. False   37. A   38. D   39. B   40. False

41. A   42. D   43. B   44. C   45. C   46. B   47. D   48. A   49. C   50. A

51. B   52. D   53. C   54. A   55. B   56. A   57. C   58. D   59. B   60. C

61. A   62. C   63. B   64. D   65. B   66. C   67. A   68. D   69. False   70. C

CHAPTER III:
NEW YORK JETS DRAFT TRIVIA
EXAM TIME

71. Ken O'Brien was drafted in the first round of the 1983 NFL draft. What college did Ken O"Brien attend?

a. USC

b. California Davis

c. Oregon

d. Penn State

72. Johnny Hector was drafted in the second round of the 1983 draft. What position did Johnny Hector play?

a. Wide Receiver

b. Tight End

c. Offensive Guard

d. Running Back

73. Reggie McElroy was drafted in the second round of the 1982 draft. What position did Reggie McElroy play?

a. Offensive Tackle

b. Offensive Guard

c. Center

d. Tight End

74. Bob Crable was drafted in the first round of the 1982 draft. What position did Bob Crable play?

a. Defensive End

b. Defensive Tackle

c. Linebacker

d. Cornerback

75. Mark Gastineau was selected in the second round of the 1979 draft. What college did Mark Gastineau attend?

a. Alabama

b. Arizona State

c. Penn State

d. Clemson

76. Marty Lyons was selected in the second round of the 1979 draft. What college did Marty Lyons attend?

a. Alabama

b. Ohio State

c. Auburn

d. USC

77. Bobby Jackson was selected in the sixth round of the 1978 draft. What position did Bobby Jackson play?

a. Linebacker

b. Cornerback

c. Safety

d. Defensive End

78. Derrick Gaffney was selected in the eighth round of the 1978 draft. What position did Derrick Gaffney play?

a. Center

b. Running Back

c. Tight End

d. Wide Receiver

79. Lance Mehl was selected in the third round of the 1978 draft. What position did Lance Mehl play?

a. Defensive End

b. Defensive Tackle

c. Linebacker

d. Cornerback

80. Ron Faurot was selected in the first round of the 1984 draft. What position did Ron Faurot play?

a. Linebacker

b. Safety

c. Defensive Tackle

d. Defensive End

81. Christian Hackenberg was a Quarterback selected by the New York Jets in the second round of the 2016 draft. Which college did Christian attend?

a. USC

b. Penn State

c. Oregon

d. Clemson

82. Devin Smith was a wide receiver selected by the New York Jets in the second round of the 2015 draft. Which college did Devin attend?

a. Ohio State

b. Alabama

c. Oklahoma

d. Oregon

83. Calvin Pryor was a safety selected by the New York Jets in the first round of the 2014 draft. Which position did Calvin play?

a. Cornerback

b. Safety

c. Linebacker

d. Defensive End

84. Geno Smith was a Quarterback selected by the New York Jets in the second round of the 2013 draft. Which college did Geno attend?

a. Alabama

b. USC

c. UCLA

d. West Virginia

85. Muhammad Wilkerson was selected by the New York Jets in the first round of the 2011 draft. What position did Muhammad play?

a. Linebacker

b. Safety

c. Defensive End

d. Cornerback

86. Bryce Hall was selected by the New York Jets in the first round of the 2020 draft. What position does Bryce play?

a. Cornerback

b. Safety

c. Linebacker

d. Defensive Tackle

87. Elijah McGuire was selected by the New York Jets in the sixth round of the 2017 draft. Which position did Elijah play?

a. Wide Receiver

b. Tight End

c. Running Back

d. Center

88. Darron Lee was an Outside Linebacker selected in the first round of the 2016 draft. What college did Darron attend?

a. Alabama

b. Clemson

c. Oklahoma

d. Ohio State

89. Jamal Adams was a Safety selected by the New York Jets in the first round of the 2017 draft. What college did Jamal attend?

a. LSU

b. Nebraska

c. UCLA

d. Clemson

90. Bilal Powell was a Running Back selected by the New York Jets in 2011. What college did Bilal attend?

a. Oregon

b. Louisville

c. USC

d. Alabama

91. Kyle Wilson was selected in the first round by the New York Jets in the 2010 draft. What position did Kyle play?

a. Linebacker

b. Safety

c. Defensive End

d. Cornerback

92. Vernon Gholston was selected by the New York Jets in the first round of the 2008 draft. What position did Vernon play?

a. Safety

b. Cornerback

c. Defensive End

d. Linebacker

93. Deon Simon was selected by the New York Jets in the seventh round of the 2015 draft. What position did Deon play?

a. Nose Tackle

b. Defensive End

c. Linebacker

d. Safety

94. Sheldon Richardson was selected by the New York Jets in the first round of the 2013 draft. What college did Sheldon attend?

a. Clemson

B. Texas

c. Missouri

d. Nebraska

95. Dustin Keller was a Tight End selected by the New York Jets in the third round of the 2008 draft. What college did Dustin attend?

a. Oregon

b. Purdue

c. Ohio State

d. USC

96. Brad Smith was a quarterback selected by the New York Jets in the 2006 draft. Which position did Brad play for the team?

a. Quarterback

b. Running Back

c. Tight End

d. Wide Receiver

97. Jonathan Vilma was selected by the New York Jets in the first round of the 2004 draft. What position did Jonathan play for the team?

a. Defensive End

b. Linebacker

c. Cornerback

d. Safety

98. Shaun Ellis was selected by the New York Jets in the first round of the 2000 draft. What position did Shaun play?

a. Defensive End

b. Linebacker

c. Cornerback

d. Safety

99. Ray Mickens was a defensive back selected by the New York Jets in 1996. In which round was Ray selected?

a. First Round

b. Second Round

c. Third Round

d. Fourth Round

100. Aaron Glenn was a defensive back selected by the New York Jets in the first round of the 1994 draft. Which college did Aaron attend?

a. Nebraska

b. Texas A & M

c. Alabama

d. Ohio State

101. Johnny Mitchell was selected in the first round of the 1992 draft. What position did Johnny play for the team?

a. Tight End

b. Wide Receiver

c. Running Back

d. Center

102. Kurt Barber was selected in the first round of the 1992 draft. What position did Kurt play for the team?

a. Defensive End

b. Defensive Tackle

c. Cornerback

d. Linebacker

103. Jeff Blake was selected in the sixth round of the 1992 draft. What position did Jeff play for the team?

a. Wide Receiver

b. Quarterback

c. Running Back

d. Tight End

104. Eric Ainge was selected by the New York Jets in the fifth round of the 2008 draft. Which position did Eric play for the team?

a. Running Back

b. Quarterback

c. Wide Receiver

d. Tight End

105. Kellen Clemens was a Quarterback selected by the New York Jets in the 2006 draft. Which college did Kellen attend?

a. Alabama

b. Nebraska

c. Oregon

d. Ohio State

106. Trenton Cannon was selected in the sixth round by the New York Jets in the 2018 draft. What position did Trenton play for the team?

a. Running back

b. Fullback

c. Wide Receiver

d. Tight End

107. ArDarius Stewart was selected in the third round by the New York Jets in the 2017 draft. What position did ArDarius play for the team?

a. Running Back

b. Tight End

c. Wide Receiver

d. Fullback

108. Brooks Bollinger was selected in the sixth round by the New York Jets in the 2003 draft. What position did Brooks play for the team?

a. Running back

b. Wide Receiver

c. Tight End

d. Quarterback

109. True or False   In the year 2000, the New York Jets had four first round draft choices.

a. True

b. False

110. Trenton Cannon was selected in the sixth round by the New York Jets in the 2018 draft. What college did Trenton attend?

a. Virginia State

b. Notre Dame

c. Alabama

d. Nebraska

111. Jace Amaro was selected in the second round by the New York Jets in 2014. What position did Jace play for the team?

a. Center

b. Wide Receiver

c. Tight End

d. Running back

112. Matt Slauson was selected in the sixth round by the New York Jets in 2009. What position did Matt play for the team?

a. Center

b. Offensive Guard

c. Tight End

d. Offensive Tackle

113. Jacob Bender was selected in the sixth round by the New York Jets in 2007. What position did Jacob play for the team?

a. Offensive Guard

b. Offensive Tackle

c. Tight End

d. Wide Receiver

114. Chris Brazzell was selected in the sixth round by the New York Jets in 1998. What position did Chris play for the team?

a. Wide receiver

b. Tight End

c. Running Back

d. Fullback

115. Kyle Brady was a Tight End selected by the New York Jets in the first round in 1995. What college did Kyle attend?

a. Oregon

b. Alabama

c. Nebraska

d. Penn State

116. Fred Baxter was a Tight End selected by the New York Jets in the fifth round of 1993. What college did Fred attend?

a. Notre Dame

b. Illinois

c. Auburn

d. Oklahoma

117. Blair Thomas was selected by the New York Jets in the first round of the 1990 draft. What position did Blair Thomas play?

a. Running Back

b. Fullback

c. Wide Receiver

d. Tight End

118. Marvin Washington was selected by the New York Jets in the sixth round of the 1989 draft. What position did Marvin play?

a. Defensive End

b. Defensive Tackle

c. Linebacker

d. Cornerback

119. James Hasty was selected by the New York Jets in the third round of the 1988 draft. What position did James play?

a. Defensive End

b. Defensive Tackle

c. Linebacker

d. Cornerback

120. Al Toon was a Wide Receiver selected by the New York Jets in the first round of the 1985 draft. What college did Al attend?

a. Clemson

b. Wisconsin

c. UCLA

d. Oregon

ANSWERS

71. B 72. D 73. A 74. C 75. B 76. A 77. B 78. D 79. C 80. D

81. B 82. A 83. B 84. D 85. C 86. A 87. C 88. D 89. A 90. B

91. D 92. C 93. A 94. C 95. B 96. D 97. B 98. A 99. C 100. B

101. A 102. D 103. B 104. B 105. C 106. A 107. C 108. D 109. True

110. A 111. C 112. B 113. B 114. A 115. D 116. C 117. A 118. A

119. True 120. B

CHAPTER IV:
New York Jets Running Back Trivia
EXAM TIME

121. Which New York Jets player leads the franchise with the greatest number of rushing yards in team history?

a. Matt Snell

b. Freeman McNeil

c. Curtis Martin

d. Emerson Boozer

122. Which New York Jets Running Back led the team in rushing yardage in the 2009 season?

a. Thomas Jones

b. Curtis Martin

c. Shonn Greene

d. LaDainian Tomlinson

123. Which New York Jets Running Back led the team in rushing yardage in the 1975 season?

a. John Riggins

b. Emerson Boozer

c. Scott Dierking

d. Clark Gaines

124. Which New York Jets Running Back led the team in rushing yardage in the 1997 season?

a. Brad Baxter

b. Adrian Murrell

c. Curtis Martin

d. Johnny Johnson

125. Which New York Jets Running Back led the team in rushing yardage in the 2009 season?

a. Chris Ivory

b. Thomas Jones

c. LaDainian Tomlinson

d. Shonn Greene

126. Which New York Jets Running Back is the third all-time leading rusher in NFL history with 16,000 yards?

a. Curtis Martin

b. Freeman McNeil

c. Frank Gore

d. Le'Veon Bell

127. Which New York Jets Running Back led the team in rushing yardage in the 2015 season?

a. Bilal Powell

b. Chris Ivory

c. Ladainian Tomlinson

d. Matt Forte

128. Johnny Hector was a Running Back for the New York Jets for 10 years. What college did Johnny attend?

a. Oregon

b. Alabama

c. Texas A & M

d. Clemson

129. Which New York Jets Running Back led the team in franchise history with the highest yards per carry average?

a. Freeman McNeil

b. Curtis Martin

c. Le'Veon Bell

d. Brad Baxter

130. Which New York Jets Running Back led the team in rushing yardage in the 2018 season?

a. Bilal Powell

b. Isaiah Crowell

c. Matt Forte

d. Chris Ivory

131. Which New York Jets Running Back led the team in rushing yardage in the 1964 season?

a. Emerson Boozer

b. Dick Christy

c. Bill Mathis

d. Matt Snell

132. Which New York Jets Running Back led the team in rushing yardage in the 1976 season?

a. Kevin Long

b. Scott Dierking

c. Clark Gaines

d. Freeman McNeil

133. Which New York Jets Running Back led the team in rushing yardage in the 1964 season?

a. Blair Thomas

b. Brad Baxter

c. Johnny Johnson

d. Adrian Murrell

134. True or False   Curtis Martin graduated from the University of Pittsburgh.

a. True

b. False

135. True or False   Danny Woodhead was a Running Back with the New York Jets and was selected in the third round of the 2008 draft.

a. True

b. False

136. True or False   Adrian Murrell was a Running back with the New York Jets and attended the college of West Virginia.

a. True

b. False

137. Adrian Murrell was a Running back with the New York Jets and was drafted in which round?

a. Third

b. Fourth

c. Fifth

d. Sixth

138. John Riggins was a Running back with the New York Jets during the 1970's. What college did John attend?

a. USC

b. University of Kansas

c. Oklahoma

d. Clemson

139. Leon Washington was a Running back with the New York Jets from 2006 – 2009. What college did Leon attend?

a. Florida State

b. Texas

c. UCLA

d. Oregon

140. LaDainian Tomlinson was a Running back with the New York Jets but was originally drafted by which team?

a. Miami Dolphins

b. Minnesota Vikings

c. Denver Broncos

d. San Diego Chargers

141. Frank Gore is a Running Back who played for the New York Jets for one season. Which NFL team drafted Frank?

a. Miami Dolphins

b. Buffalo Bills

c. San Francisco 49ers

d. Indianapolis Colts

142. Curtis Martin was a Running Back who played for the New York Jets for 8 seasons. Which team drafted Curtis?

a. Philadelphia Eagles

b. New England Patriots

c. New Orleans Saints

d. Pittsburgh Steelers

143. Chris Ivory was a Running Back who played for the New York Jets for 3 seasons. Which team drafted Chris?

a. Miami Dolphins

b. Buffalo bills

c. New Orleans Saints

d. Atlanta Falcons

144. Isaiah Crowell was a Running Back who played for the New York Jets for one season. Which team drafted Isaiah?

a. Cleveland Browns

b. New England Patriots

c. Minnesota Vikings

d. Denver Broncos

145. True or False   Le'Veon Bell rushed for over 1,000 yards in 2019 for the New York Jets.

a. True

b. False

146. Blair Thomas was a Running Back for the New York Jets for 4 seasons. Which round of the 1990 draft was Blair selected?

a. First

b. Second

c. Third

d. Fourth

147. Matt Forte was a Running Back for the New York Jets for 2 seasons. Which team drafted Matt?

a. Minnesota Vikings

b. Denver Broncos

c. Chicago Bears

d. New England Patriots

148. Michael Carter is a Running Back and was drafted in 2021 by the New York Jets. What college did Michael attend?

a. Arkansas

b. North Carolina

c. Florida State

d. Clemson

149. Johnny Johnson was a Running back for the New York Jets for two seasons. Which team drafted Johnny?

a. New York Giants

b. Phoenix Cardinals

c. New England Patriots

d. Pittsburgh Steelers

150. Tommy Bohanon was a Fullback selected by the New York Jets in the 2013 draft. What college did Tommy attend?

a. Penn State

b. Florida State

c. Clemson

d. Wake Forest

ANSWERS

121. C 122. A 123. A 124. B 125. D 126. C 127. B
128. C 129. A 130. B

131. D 132. C 133. A 134. True 135. False 136. True

137. C 138. B 139. A 140. D 141. C 142. B 143. C

144. A 145. False 146. A 147. C 148. B 149. B

150. D

CHAPTER V:
NEW YORK JETS QUARTERBACK TRIVIA
EXAM TIME

151. Since Joe Namath, how many quarterbacks have the New York Jets had since he left the team?

a. Twenty

b. Twenty five

c. Thirty

d. Thirty five

152. Who was the starting quarterback for the New York Jets in 1960?

a. Al Dorow

b. Dick Wood

C. Johnny Green

d. Pete Liske

153. Who was the starting quarterback for the New York Jets in 1963?

a. Dick Wood

b. Galen Hall

c. Al Woodall

d. Pete Liske

154. Who was the starting quarterback for the New York Jets in 1970?

a. Mike Taliaferro

b. Al Woodall

c. Galen Hall

d. Bob Davis

155. This player was the starting quarterback for the New York Jets in 2000. He also won the Heisman Trophy award in 1986. Who was this great quarterback?

a. Rick Mirer

b. Glenn Foley

c. Bubby Brister

d. Vinny Testaverde

156. Neil O'Donnell was the starting quarterback for the New York Jets in 1997. Which three other teams did he play for?

a. Vikings, Saints, and Bears

b. Steelers, Bengals, and Titans

c. Giants, Browns, and Saints

d. Eagles, Falcons, and Dolphins

157. In 2017, who was the New York Jets starting quarterback?

a. Josh McCown

b. Sam Darnold

c. Geno Smith

d. Ryan Fitzpatrick

158. Michael Vick was a free agent acquisition acquired by the New York Jets in 2014. Which other teams did Michael Vick play for?

a. Miami Dolphins and Philadelphia Eagles

b. Philadelphia Eagles and Denver Broncos

c. Atlanta Falcons and Philadelphia Eagles

d. New England Patriots and New Orleans Saints

159. Brett Favre was a free agent acquired by the New York Jets in 2008. Which other teams did Brett Favre play for?

a. Cincinnati Bengals and Minnesota Vikings

b. Green Bay Packers and Buffalo Bills

c. Minnesota Vikings and Houston Texans

d. Green Bay Packers and Minnesota Vikings

160. Chad Pennington was drafted in the first round of 2000 by the New York Jets. Which other team did Chad play for in the NFL?

a. New England Patriots

b. Buffalo Bills

c. Miami Dolphins

d. Philadelphia Eagles

161. How many interceptions did Geno Smith throw in 2013?

a. 19

b. 21

c. 23

d. 25.

162. What is Chad Pennington's playoff record?

a. 2 wins, 3 losses

b. 3 wins, 2 losses

c. 4 wins, 1 loss

d. 0 wins, 5 losses

163. How many wins does Mark Sanchez have in the playoffs?

a. 2

b. 3

c. 4

d. 5

164. How many years did New York Jets quarterback Mark Sanchez play in the NFL?

a. 7 years

b. 8 years

c. 9 years

d. 10 years

165. What was Mark Sanchez's record in the NFL?

a. 35 wins and 38 losses

b. 37 wins and 36 losses

c. 30 wins and 43 losses

d. 32 wins and 41 losses

166. Who was the backup quarterback for Chad Pennington for three games in the 2004 season?

a. Rick Mirer

b. Quincy Carter

c. Brooks Bollinger

d. Kellen Clemens

167. Chad Pennington was the starting quarterback for the New York Jets in the 2004 Wild Card Game. Which team did the New York Jets play in that game?

a. New England Patriots

b. Pittsburgh Steelers

c. Baltimore Ravens

d. San Diego Chargers

168. How many interceptions did Richard Todd throw in the playoff game against the Buffalo Bills?

a. 4

b. 3

c. 2

d. 1

169. Which New York Jets quarterback beat the Kansas City Chiefs in the 1986 Wild Card Game?

a. Ken O'Brien

b. Richard Todd

c. Pat Ryan

d. Tony Eason

170. How many interceptions did Joe Namath throw in the 1969 Wild Card Game against the Kansas City Chiefs?

a. 3

b. 2

c. 1

d. 0

171. True or False   Ken O"Brien began his rookie year of 1983 as the starting quarterback of the New York Jets.

a. True

b. False

172. True or False   New York Jets quarterback Matt Robinson was drafted in the ninth round of the 1977 draft?

a. True

b. False

173. What was New York Jets quarterback Joe Namath's record with the team in 1968?

a. 8 wins and 6 losses

b. 9 wins and 5 losses

c. 10 wins and 4 losses

d. 11 wins and 3 losses

174. What was New York Jets quarterback Ken O'Brien's record with the team in 1984?

a. 3 wins and 2 losses

b. 2 wins and 2 losses

c. 1 win and 3 losses

d. 0 wins and 4 losses

175. What was New York Jets quarterback Geno Smith's record with the team in 2013?

a. 9 wins and 7 losses

b. 8 wins and 8 losses

c. 7 wins and 9 losses

d. 6 wins and 10 losses

176. After Joe Namath, which quarterback is second in career passing yards with the New York Jets?

a. Ken O'Brien

b. Richard Todd

c. Chad Pennington

d. Vinny Testaverde

177. Ryan Fitzpatrick was the quarterback for the New York Jets in 2015 and 2016. How many total teams did Ryan play for in his career?

a. 5

b. 6

c. 7

d. 8

178. How many touchdown passes did Vinny Testaverde throw in his first year with the New York Jets?

a. 23

b. 26

c. 29

d. 31

179. What was Brett Favre's record with the New York Jets in his first and only year with the team?

a. 7 wins and 4 losses

b. 8 wins and 3 losses

c. 9 wins and 2 losses

d. 10 wins and 1 loss

180. How many touchdown passes did Brett Favre throw with the New York Jets in 2008?

a. 18

b. 20

c. 22

d. 24

ANSWERS

151. D 152. A 153. A 154. B 155. D 156. B 157. A
158. C 159. D 160. C

161. B 162. A 163. C 164. D 165. B 166. B 167. D
168. A 169. C 170. A

171. False 172. True 173. D 174. C 175. B 176. A 177.
D 178. C 179. B

180. C

CHAPTER VI:
NEW YORK JETS SACK LEADERS TRIVIA
EXAM TIME

181. In 2013, which New York Jets defensive lineman led the team in sacks?

a. John Abraham

b. Muhammad Wilkerson

c. Jordan Jenkins

d. Sheldon Richardson

182. Dennis Byrd led the New York Jets in sacks in 1990. How many sacks did he have in that season?

a. 9

b. 11

c. 13

d. 15

183. Shaun Ellis led the New York Jets in sacks in 2003. How many sacks did he have in that season?

a. 12.5

b. 10.5

c. 8.5

d. 6.5

184. Mo Lewis led the New York Jets in sacks in 2000. How many sacks did he have in that season?

a. 8

b. 10

c. 12

d. 14

185. Which New York Jets player led the team in sacks in 1995?

a. Jeff Lagerman

b. Dennis Byrd

c. Marvin Washington

d. Hugh Douglas

186. Which New York Jets player led the team in sacks in 2009?

a. Shaun Ellis

b. Victor Hobson

c. Calvin Pace

d. Sione Pouha

187. Which New York Jets player led the team in sacks in 2006?

a. Bryan Thomas

b. Shaun Ellis

c. Brian Cox

d. Josh Evans

188. Which New York Jets player led the team in sacks in 1983, 1984, and 1985?

a. Marty Lyons

b. Mark Gastineau

c. Joe Klecko

d. Barry Bennett

189. Which two New York Jets players were tied for the team in sacks in 2018?

a. Jordan Jenkins and Henry Anderson

b. Jamal Adams and Jordan Jenkins

c. Leonard Williams and Muhammad Wilkerson

d. Leonard Williams and Jordan Jenkins

190. Which New York Jets defensive lineman led the league in sacks in 1984?

a. John Abraham

b. Joe Klecko

c. Abdul Salaam

d. Mark Gastineau

191. Which college did New York Jets defensive lineman Hugh Douglas attend?

a. USC

b. Oregon

c. Central State

d. UCLA

192. How many sacks did Barry Bennett have in his career for the New York Jets?

a. 12.5

b. 14.5

c. 16.5

d. 18.5

193. Which linebacker had the most sacks in his career for the New York Jets?

a. Lance Mehl

b. Mo Lewis

c. David Harris

d. Bryan Cox

194. Which New York Jets player is the second leader in sacks in team history?

a. Shaun Ellis

b. John Abraham

c. Mo Lewis

d. Calvin Pace

195. Which New York Jets defensive back is the leader in sacks in team history?

a. Kerry Rhodes

b. Jamal Adams

c .Victor Green

d. Darrelle Revis

196. How many sacks did Jamal Adams have with the New York Jets?

a. 3

b. 6

c. 9

d. 12

197. How many sacks did Mo Lewis have in his career with the New York Jets?

a. 32.5

b. 42.5

c. 52.5

d. 62.5

198. Which college did New York Jets defensive lineman Shaun Ellis attend?

a. Tennessee

b. UCLA

c. Auburn

d. Notre Dame

199. How many sacks did John Abraham have in his career with the New York Jets?

a. 33.5

b. 43.5

c. 53.5

d. 63.5

200. Mark Gastineau was drafted in what round of the 1979 draft?

a. First

b. Second

c. Third

d. Fourth

201. Shaun Ellis was drafted in what round of the 1979 draft?

a. First

b. Second

c. Third

d. Fourth

202. True or False John Abraham was drafted in the second round of the 2000 draft?

a. True

b. False

203. In what year did John Abraham have the most sacks in his career with the New York Jets?

a. 2001

b. 2008

c. 2010

d. 2013

204. What was the highest number of sacks Mo Lewis had with the New York Jets in a given season?

a. 4

b. 6

c. 8

d. 10

205. What was the highest number of sacks Muhammad Wilkerson had with the New York Jets in a given season?

a. 10

b. 12

c. 14

d. 16

206. What was the highest number of sacks John Abraham had with the New York Jets in a given season?

a. 13

b. 14

c. 15

d. 16

207. What was the highest number of sacks Marvin Washington had with the New York Jets in a given season?

a. 4.5

b. 6.5

c. 8.5

d. 10.5

208. What was the highest number of sacks Shaun Ellis had with the New York Jets in a given season?

a. 6.5

b. 8.5

c. 10.5

d. 12.5

209. What was the highest number of sacks Dennis Byrd had with the New York Jets in a given season?

a. 11

b. 13

c. 15

d. 17

210. What was the highest number of sacks Hugh Douglas had with the New York Jets in a given season?

a. 9

b. 10

c. 11

d. 12

211. How many touchdowns did running back Blair Thomas have with the New York Jets?

a. 5

b. 10

c. 15

d. 20

212. Brandon Moore was a defensive tackle coming into the NFL. What position did he play for with the New York Jets?

a. Defensive End

b. Linebacker

c. Offensive Tackle

d. Offensive Guard

213. Which New York Jets player suffered a life threatening and career ending injury in a game with the team?

a. Joe Klecko

b. Dennis Byrd

c. Scott Mersereau

d. Bobby Jackson

214. Which position did Trevor Siemian play for the New York Jets?

a. Running Back

b. Tight End

c. Quarterback

d. Wide Receiver

215. Which position did New York Jets player Brad Smith play in college?

a. Wide Receiver

b. Quarterback

c. Tight End

d. Running Back

216. What position does New York Jets undrafted free agent Kyron Brown play?

a. Cornerback

b. Safety

c. Linebacker

d. Defensive Tackle

217. What position does New York Jets undrafted free agent Camilo Eifler play?

a. Defensive End

b. Defensive Tackle

c. Cornerback

d. Linebacker

218. What position does New York Jets undrafted free agent Javelin Guidry play?

a. Safety

b. Cornerback

c. Linebacker

d. Defensive Tackle

219. What position does New York Jets undrafted free agent Lawrence Cager play?

a. Running Back

b. Tight End

c. Wide Receiver

d. Center

220. What position does New York Jets undrafted free agent Hamilcar Rashed Jr. play?

a. Cornerback

b. Safety

c. Linebacker

d. Defensive End

ANSWERS

181. B   182. C   183. A   184. B   185. D   186. C   187. A
188. B   189. A   190. D

191. C   192. D   193. B   194. A   195. B   196. D   197. C
198. A   199. C   200. B

201. A   202. False   203. B   204. D   205. B   206. A   207. C
208. D   209. B   210. B

211. A   212. D   213. B   214. C   215. B   216. A   217. D
218. B   219. C   220. D

CHAPTER VII:
New York Jet Pro Bowl and Hall of Famers Trivia
EXAM TIME

221. True or False   New York Jets player Mark Gastineau was elected to the Pro Football Hall of Fame.

a. True

b. False

222. True or False   New York Jets running back LaDainian Tomlinson was elected to the Pro Football Hall of Fame.

a. True

b. False

223. Al Dorow was selected to one Pro Bowl? Which position did Al Dorow play?

a. Running back

b. Quarterback

c. Wide Receiver

d. Tight End

224. New York Jets player Mickey Shuler was selected to two Pro Bowls. What position did Mickey play?

a. Quarterback

b. Running Back

c. Wide Receiver

d. Tight End

225. New York Jets player John Elliott was selected to three Pro Bowls. What position did John play?

a. Defensive Tackle

b. Linebacker

c. Cornerback

d. Safety

226. New York Jets player Richie Anderson was selected to one Pro Bowl. What position did Richie play?

a. Running Back

b. Fullback

c. Wide Receiver

d. Tight End

227. New York Jets player Bake Turner was selected to one Pro Bowl. What position did Bake play?

a. Wide Receiver

b. Running Back

c. Tight End

d. Quarterback

228. New York Jets player Justin Miller was selected to one Pro Bowl. What position did Justin play?

a. Defensive Tackle

b. Linebacker

c. Safety

d. Cornerback

229. True or False   Brandon Marshall was selected to two Pro Bowls in his career with the New York Jets.

a. True

b. False

230. Alan Faneca was selected to two Pro Bowls with the New York Jets. What position did Alan play?

a. Wide Receiver

b. Center

c. Offensive Guard

d. Fullback

231. Joe Namath of the New York Jets was selected to how many Pro Bowls?

a. 2

b. 3

c. 4

d. 5

232. Freeman McNeil of the New York Jets was selected to how many Pro Bowls?

a. 1

b. 2

c. 3

d. 4

233. Leon Washington of the New York Jets was selected to how many Pro Bowls?

a. 1

b. 2

c. 3

d. 4

234. One New York Jets Head coach was elected to the Pro Football Hall of Fame. Which New York Jets Head coach was elected?

a. Joe Walton

b. Herm Edwards

c. Weeb Ewbank

d. Bruce Coslet

235. Which Offensive Tackle of the New York Jets was elected to the Pro Football Hall of Fame?

a. Marvin Powell

b. Winston Hill

c. Sherman Plunkett

d. D'Brickashaw Ferguson

236. Which New York Jets wide receiver was elected to the Pro Football Hall of Fame?

a. Don Maynard.

b. Al Toon

c. Wesley Walker

d. George Sauer

237. Which New York Jets safety was elected to the Pro Football Hall of Fame?

a. Victor Green

b. Erik McMillan

c. Kerry Rhodes

d. Ed Reed

238. True or False   Joe Klecko was selected to the Pro Bowl two times.

a. True

b. False

239. True or False   Pat Leahy was selected to the Pro Bowl one time.

a. True

b. False

240. Which New York Jets linebacker was selected to five Pro Bowls in the 1960's?

a. Roger Ellis

b. Larry Grantham

c. Eddie Bell

d. Ralph Baker

241. Which New York Jets center was selected to seven Pro Bowls in his career?

a. Joe Fields

b. Kevin Mawae

c. Nick Mangold

d. Jim Sweeney

242. Which New York Jets cornerback was selected to five Pro Bowls in his career?

a. Darelle Revis

b. Antonio Cromartie

c. Aaron Glenn

d. Justin Miller

243. Which New York Jets quarterback was selected to five Pro Bowls in his career?

a. Boomer Esiason

b. Vinny Testaverde

c. Ken O'Brien

d. Joe Namath

244. Which New York Jets defensive end was selected to five Pro Bowls in his career?

a. Joe Klecko

b. Mark Gastineau

c. Gerry Philbin

d. John Abraham

245. Which New York Jets offensive tackle was selected to eight Pro Bowls in his career?

a. Winston Hill

b. Marvin Powell

c. D'Bricksashaw Ferguson

d. Sherman Plunkett

246. Which New York Jets safety was selected to two Pro Bowls in his career?

a. Victor Green

b. Erik McMillan

c. Jamal Adams

d. Marcus Maye

247. Which New York Jets quarterback was selected to the Pro Bowl in 1999?

a. Ray Lucas

b. Vinny Testaverde

c. Tom Tupa

d. Boomer Esiason

248. Which New York Jets offensive tackle was selected to the Pro Bowl five times in his career?

a. Sherman Plunkett

b. Marvin Powell

c. D'Brickashaw Ferguson

d. Dan Alexander

249. Which New York Jets linebacker was selected to the Pro Bowl three times in his career?

a. Mo Lewis

b. Joe Kelly

c. Lance Mehl

d. Jonathan Vilma

250. Which New York Jets wide receiver was selected four consecutive years to the Pro Bowl in his career?

a. Wesley Walker

b. George Sauer

c. Don Maynard

d. Keyshawn Johnson

251. What college did Hall of Famer Winston Hill attend?

a. Michigan

b. Ohio Sate

c. Texas Southern

d. Baylor

252. John Riggins was selected to how many Pro Bowl games?

a. 0

b. 1

c. 2

d. 3

253. Marvin Powell was selected to how many Pro Bowls?

a. 2

b. 3

c. 4

d. 5

254. What year was Curtis Martin inducted into the Pro Football Hall Of Fame?

a. 2012

b. 2015

c. 2018

d. 2020

255. What other New York Jets Running Back besides Curtis Martin was inducted into the Pro Football Hall of Fame?

a. Freeman McNeil

b. John Riggins

c. Emerson Boozer

d. Matt Snell

256. What year was Joe Namath inducted into the Pro Football Hall of Fame?

a. 1983

b. 1985

c. 1987

d. 1989

257. Who was the only New York Jets Fullback to be selected to the Pro Bowl for two years in their career?

a. Tony Richardson

b. Roger Vick

c. Bill Mathis

d. Tommy Bohanon

258. True or False   Joe Klecko of the New York Jets was inducted into the Pro Football Hall of Fame in 1995.

a. True

b. False

259. True or False   LaRon Landry was a Linebacker with the New York Jets and was selected one time to the Pro Bowl.

a. True

b. False

260. True or False Ken O'Brien was selected to two Pro Bowls in his career with the New York Jets.

a. True

b. False

ANSWERS

221. False 222. True 223. B 224. D 225. A 226. B 227. B 228. D 229. False

230. C 231. D 232. C 233. A 234. C 235. B 236. A 237. D 238. False

239. False   240. B   241. C   242. A   243. D   244. D   245. A
246. C   247. C   248. B

249. A   250. B   251. C   252. B   253. D   254. A   255. B
256. B   257. C   258. False

259. False   260. True

CHAPTER VIII:
NEW YORK JETS RECEIVING LEADERS TRIVIA
EXAM TIME

261. True or False   New York Jets receiving leader Don Maynard also played for the New York Giants.

a. True

b. False

262. In which round was New York Jets receiving leader Wesley Walker selected in the 1977 draft?

a. First

b. Second

c. Third

d. Fourth

263. How many yards did receiving leader Wayne Chrebet have for the New York Jets?

a. 7,300 yards

b. 8,300 yards

c. 9,300 yards

d. 10,300 yards

264. In which round was receiving leader Al Toon selected in the 1985 draft?

a. First

b. Second

c. Third

d. Fourth

265. In which round was receiving leader Laverneus Coles selected in the 2000   draft?

a. First

b. Second

c. Third

d. Fourth

266. How many years did New York Jets receiving leader George Sauer play for the New York Jets?

a. 4

b. 6

c. 8

d. 10

267. Mickey Shuler was a receiving leader for the New York Jets. What other team did Mickey play for?

a. Miami Dolphins

b. Denver Broncos

c. Seattle Seahawks

d. Philadelphia Eagles

268. Don Maynard is a receiving leader for the New York Jets. What other team did Don play for?

a. Chicago Bears

b. St. Louis Cardinals

c. New York Giants

d. Oakland Raiders

269. True or False   Keyshawn Johnson played for three other NFL teams besides the New York Jets.

a. True

b. False

270. Which New York Jets wide receiver holds the record for the most receiving yards in a season?

a. Eric Decker

b. Al Toon

c, Laverneus Coles

d. Brandon Marshall

271. How many years did New York Jets receiving leader Al Toon play for the New York Jets?

a. 6

b. 8

c. 10

d. 12

272. Besides the New York Jets, receiving leader Eric Decker played for two other NFL teams. Which other teams did Eric play for?

a. Miami Dolphins and Philadelphia Eagles

b. New England Patriots and Denver Broncos

c. Tennessee Titans and Pittsburgh Steelers

d. Denver Broncos and Tennessee Titans

273. Which wide receiver is in second place in season receiving yards for the New York Jets?

a. Leveranues Coles

b. Keyshawn Johnson

c. Don Maynard

d. Richie Anderson

274. Which wide receiver is in third place in season receiving yards for the New York Jets?

a. Wayne Chrebet

b. Richie Anderson

c. Al Toon

d. Keyshawn Johnson

275. Which New York Jets receiver has the longest yards per play (one play) in team history?

a. Al Toon

b. Richie Anderson

c. Don Maynard

d. Wesley Walker

276. Which teams did Laveranues Coles play for besides the New York Jets?

a. Washington and Cincinnati

b. Miami and New England

c. Cleveland and Philadelphia

d. Seattle and Denver

277. Which New York Jets receiving leader led the team in yards per catch (total receiving history with the team) in franchise history?

a. Don Maynard

b. Wesley Walker

c. Al Toon

d. Wayne Chrebet

278. Which college did New York Jets receiving leader George Sauer attend?

a. UCLA

b. USC

c. Oregon

d. Texas

279. Which college did New York Jets receiving leader Al Toon attend?

a. Texas

b. Wisconsin

c. Ohio State

d. Nebraska

280. Who was the second Tight End in receiving yards for the New York Jets in team history?

a. Mickey Shuler

b. Richard Caster

c. Jerome Barkum

d. Dustin Keller

281. In what round was New York Jets Tight End Jerome Barkum selected in the NFL draft?

a. First

b. Second

c. Third

d. Fourth

282. In what round was New York Jets Tight End Mickey Shuler selected in the NFL draft?

a. First

b. Second

c. Third

d. Fourth

283. What college did New York Jets receiving leader Mickey Shuler attend?

a. Ohio State

b. Penn State

c. Alabama

d. Nebraska

284. What college did New York Jets receiving leader Don Maynard attend?

a. Notre Dame

b. Alabama

c. Texas El Paso

d. Florida State

285. Which two teams did Wide Receiver Jericho Cotchery play for besides the New York Jets?

a. New England Patriots and Pittsburgh Steelers

b. Carolina Panthers and Miami Dolphins

c. Seattle Seahawks and Philadelphia Eagles

d. Pittsburgh Steelers and Carolina Panthers

286. In which round was Fullback Richie Anderson drafted?

a. Sixth Round

b. Fifth Round

c. Fourth Round

d. Third Round

287. Which team did Wide Receiver Santana Moss play for besides the New York Jets?

a. Denver Broncos

b. Seattle Seahawks

c. Houston Texans

d. Washington Redskins

288. Wide receiver Bake Turner played for one other team besides the New York Jets? Which other team did Bake play for?

a. Philadelphia Eagles

b. Atlanta Falcons

c. Boston Patriots

d. Oakland Raiders

289. Wide receiver Rob Moore played for one other team besides the New York Jets? Which other team did Rob play for?

a. New England patriots

b. Arizona Cardinals

c. New York Giants

d. Pittsburgh Steelers

290. Wide receiver Jeremy Kerley played for two other teams besides the New York Jets? Which other teams did Jeremy play for?

a. San Francisco 49ers and Buffalo Bills

b. New Orleans Saints and Philadelphia Eagles

c. Buffalo Bills and Washington Redskins

d. Pittsburgh Steelers and Houston Texans

ANSWERS

261. True 262. B 263. A 264. A 265. C 266. B 267. D
268. B 269. True 270. D 271. B 272. D 273. C 274. A
275. D 276. A 277. B 278. D 279. B

280. C 281. A 282. C 283. B 284. C 285. D 286. A
287. D 288. C 289. B

290. A

CHAPTER IX:
NEW YORK JETS HEAD COACHES AND GM TRIVIA
EXAM TIME

291. Who was the New York Jets first Head Coach?

a. Bulldog Turner

b. Sammy Baugh

c. Weeb Ewbank

d. Ken Shipp

292. Which New York Jets Head Coach had the highest win loss percentage of all coaches in team history?

a. Bill Parcells

b. Al Groh

c. Joe Walton

d. Weeb Ewbank

293. Which New York Jets Head Coach won the most games for the team in franchise history?

a. Joe Walton

b. Weeb Ewbank

c. Rex Ryan

d. Walt Michaels

294. Which New York Jets Head Coach brought his team to the AFC Championship game two years in a row?

a. Bruce Coslet

b. Walt Michaels

c. Joe Walton

d. Rex Ryan

295. Which New York Jets head Coach brought his team to the playoffs the most times?

a. Rex Ryan

b. Eric Mangini

c. Herm Edwards

d. Joe Walton

296. How many Head Coaches did the New York Jets have in their team history?

a. 14

b. 16

c. 18

d. 20

297. Which are the only two New York Jets Head Coaches that had a winning record with the team?

a. Bill Parcells and Al Groh

b. Joe Walton and Walt Michaels

c. Eric Mangini and Herm Edwards

d. Weeb Ewbank and Wwalt Michaels

298. True or False   Al Groh coached for both the New York Jets and New York Giants.

a. True

b. False

299. True or False   Head Coach Eric Mangini was also an Offensive Coordinator for the New England Patriots.

a. True

b. False

300. Bruce Coslet was a Head Coach for one other team besides the New York Jets. Which other team did he coach?

a. Cincinnati Bengals

b. Dallas Cowboys

c. Seattle Seahawks

d. Atlanta Falcons

301. Head Coach Walt Michaels worked for one other team as a Defensive Coordinator. Which other team did Walt Michaels work for?

a. Miami Dolphins

b. Dallas Cowboys

c. Oakland Raiders

d. Philadelphia Eagles

302. True or False   Joe Walton was a Head Coach of the New York Jets and Pittsburgh Steelers.

a. True

b. False

303. Who was the GM of the New York Jets when Todd Bowles was the Head Coach?

a. John Idzik

b. Mike McCagnan

c. Terry Bradway

d. Mike Tannebaum

304. True or False   Pete Carroll coached the New York Jets for two years.

a. True

b. False

305. Which two teams besides the New York Jets did Pete Carroll serve as Head Coach?

a. Seattle Seahawks and Cleveland Browns

b. Seattle Seahawks and Atlanta Falcons

c. Seattle Seahawks and Jacksonville Jaguars

d. Seattle Seahawks and New England Patriots

306. New York Jets Head Coach Sammy Baugh coached the New York Titans for two seasons. What position did Sammy play in college?

a. Wide Receiver

b. Quarterback

c. Tight End

d. Center

307. Head Coach Charley Winner of the New York Jets also coached one other team in the NFL. Which other team did Charley Winner serve as Head Coach?

a. Philadelphia Eagles

b. Dallas Cowboys

c. Baltimore Colts

d. Seattle Seahawks

308. Head Coach Rex Ryan coached one other team besides the New York Jets. Which other team did Rex Ryan coach?

a. Buffalo Bills

b. Atlanta Falcons

c. Detroit Lions

d. North Carolina Panthers

309. Which New York Jets Head Coach had the lowest win loss percentage in team history?

a. Adam Gase

b. Rich Kotite

c. Lou Holtz

d. Bulldog Turner

310. This New York Jets Head Coach was also an assistant with the Chicago Bears.

Who was this Head Coach?

a. Ken Shipp

b. Charley Winner

c. Todd Bowles

d. Bulldog Turner

311. True or False   Head Coach Bill Parcells was also the General Manager of the team during his tenure with the New York Jets.

a. True

b. False

312. Head Coach Adam Gase was also the Offensive Coordinator for which teams?

a. Denver Broncos and Chicago Bears

b. Minnesota Vikings and Washington Redskins

c. Seattle Seahawks and Green Bay Packers

d. Atlanta Falcons and Jacksonville Jaguars

313. Head Coach Mike Holovak only coached one game with the New York Jets. What other team was he the Head Coach for eight years?

a. Green Bay Packers

b. Boston Patriots

c. Philadelphia Eagles

d. Oakland Raiders

314. Which teams besides the New York Jets was Bill Parcells their Head Coach?

a. New York Giants, New England Patriots and Philadelphia Eagles

b. New York Giants, Denver Broncos and New England Patriots

c. New York Giants, New England Patriots and Atlanta Falcons

d. New York Giants, New England Patriots and Dallas Cowboys

315. Who was the Offensive Coordinator for Head Coach Bill Parcells?

a. Charlie Weis

b. Paul Hackett

c. Dan Henning

d. Brian Schottenheimer

316. New Jets Head Coach Robert Saleh worked for four other teams in a defensive capacity. Which other teams was he affiliated with?

a. 49ers, Eagles Jaguars and Texans

b. 49ers, Vikings, Jaguars and Texans

c. 49ers, Saints, Jaguars and Texans

d. 49ers, Jaguars, Seahawks and Texans

317. True or False   Head Coach Al Groh coached the New York Jets for one year.

A. True

b. False

318. Head Coach Ken Shipp coached the New York Jets for six games. Which three other teams did he serve as Offensive Coordinator?

a. Houston Oilers, Detroit Lions and Cleveland Browns

b. Houston Oilers, New Orleans Saints and Detroit Lions

c. Houston Oilers, Dallas Cowboys and Detroit Lions

d. Houston Oilers, Miami Dolphins and Detroit Lions

319. New York Jets Head Coach Weeb Ewbank also coached for one other NFL team. Which other team did Weeb Ewbank serve as Head Coach?

a. Baltimore Colts

b. Kansas City Chiefs

c. Oakland Raiders

d. Detroit Lions

320. Who will be the new Offensive Coordinator for the New York Jets in 2021?

a. Chan Gailey

b. John Morton

c. Mike LaFleur

d. Jeremy Bates

ANSWERS

291. B   292. A   293. B   294. D   295. C   296. D   297. A
298. True   299. False   300. A   301. D   302. False   303. B
304. False   305. D   306. B   307. C   308. A

309. B   310. D   311. True   312. A   313. B   314. D   315. A
316. D   317. True

318. B   319. A   320. C

CHAPTER X:
NEW YORK JETS GREATEST PLAYMAKERS TRIVIA
EXAM TIME

321. Which New York Jets player lead the team in interceptions in team history?

a. Darelle Revis

b. Victor Green

c. Bill Baird

d. Antonio Cromartie

322. This New York Jets defensive player has the most interception return yards in team history. Who is this New York Jets interception return yards leader?

a. Victor Green

b. Erik McMillan

c. Burgess Owens

d. Darrol Ray

323. This New York Jets defensive player has the longest interception yard return in franchise history. Who is the player who achieved this feat?

a. Aaron Glenn

b. Marcus Coleman

c. Darrelle Revis

d. Marcus Maye

324. This New York Jets Wide Receiver had five 1,000 yard seasons and 50 one hundred yard games. This player's record still has not been broken today as of 2021. Who is this great player?

a. Wesley Walker

b. Al Toon

c. Don Maynard

d. George Sauer

325. This New York Jets running back amassed 10, 302 yards in his career and also had seven 1,000 yard seasons with the team. Who is this great running back?

a. Freeman McNeil

b. Curtis Martin

c. Emerson Boozer

d. Matt Snell

326. This New York Jets offensive lineman was selected to the Pro Bowl for six consecutive years. He paved the way for one of the greatest running backs in team history. Who was this great offensive lineman?

a. Kevin Mawae

b. Joe Fields

c. Nick Mangold

d. Randy Rasmussen

327. This New York Jets defender was selected to three straight Pro Bowls. He also is the all-time leader in tackles and had 29 forced fumbles in his career. Who is this great defensive player?

a. Mark Gastineau

b. Joe Klecko

c. Mo Lewis

d. Greg Buttle

328. This New York Jets defensive player played in 170 games on the defensive line, a team record. He also achieved 72.5 sacks in his career, third in team history. Who is this great New York Jets defender?

a. Shaun Ellis

b. Calvin Pace

c. John Abraham

d. Muhammad Wilkerson

329. This New York Jets player has 517 career receptions and is fourth all time in reception yards for the team. He also was selected to three consecutive Pro Bowls and was inducted into the New York Jets Ring of Honor. Who is this great receiver?

a. Al Toon

b. Wesley Walker

c. Johnny Lam Jones

d. Wayne Chrebet

330. This great defensive player only played six years with the New York Jets. If he continued to play for the team, he would have been the team sack leader. In his time with the team, he was selected to 3 Pro Bowls, had 19 forced fumbles, and averaged 9 sacks per season. Who is this great defensive player?

a. Mark Gastineau

b. Marty Lyons

c. Abdul Saalam

d. John Abraham

331. This great New York Jets Offensive Lineman was selected to 8 Pro Bowls. He was part of an offensive line that allowed the fewest sacks and supported the most rushing touchdowns in a season. Who is this great offensive lineman?

a. Marvin Powell

b. Nck Mangold

c. Winston Hill

d. Randy Rasmussen

332. This great New York Jets player was selected to 4 Pro Bowls. He also had 20.5 sacks in one year and a total of 77 sacks in his career. Who is this great defensive player?

a. Mark Gastineau

b. Joe Klecko

c. John Abraham

d. Shaun Ellis

333. This great New York Jets defender had 24 interceptions with the team along with a 100 yard interception return. Who is this great New York Jets defender?

a. Marcus Coleman

b. Johnny Lynn

c. Darrelle Revis

d. Aaron Glenn

334. This great New York Jets defender had 29 interceptions with the team in his career along with 343 return yards, sixth in team history. Who is this great New York Jets defender?

a. Darrol Ray

b. Erik McMillan

c. Dainard Paulson

d. Antonio Cromartie

335. This great New York Jets defender has the most touchdowns scored off of an interception in team history with five. Who is this great New York Jets defender?

a. Victor Green

b. Erik McMillan

c. Darrelle Revis

d. Marcus Coleman

336. This great New York Jets defender is second in return yards off of an interception in team history with 581 yards. Who is this great New York Jets defender?

a. Darrol Ray

b. Marcus Coleman

c. James Hasty

d. Johnny Lynn

337. This great New York Jets defender had 24 career interceptions with the team. Who is this great New York Jets defender?

a. Burgess Owens

b. Johnny Lynn

c. Marcus Coleman

d. Larry Grantham

338. This great New York Jets defender had 25 career interceptions, and a 100 yard interception return with the team. Who is this great New York Jets defender?

a. Antonio Cromartie

b. Darrelle Revis

c. Darrol Ray

d. Marcus Coleman

339. This great New York Jets defender achieved 10 career interceptions in only 23 games along with a 74 yard interception return. Who is this great New York Jets defender?

a. Ty Law

b.Marcus Turner

c. Jerry Holmes

d. Rich Sowells

340. This great New York Jets defender achieved 15 career interceptions in only 26 games. Who is this great New York Jets defender?

a. Johnny Sample

b. Jim Hudson

c. Lee Riley

d. W. K. Hicks

ANSWERS

321. C   322. B   323. D   324. C   325. B   326. A   327. C
328. A   329. A   330. D

331. C   332. B   333. D   334. C   335. B   336. A   337. D
338. B   339. A   340. C

CHAPTER XI:
NEW YORK JETS SEASON STATS LEADERS
EXAM TIME

341. Which New York Jets defender had the most tackles in the 2021 season?

a. Bless Austin

b. Harvey Langi

c. Neville Hewitt

d. Avery Williamson

342. Which New York Jets player led the team in interceptions in 2019?

a. Morris Claiborne

b. Trumaine Johnson

c. Darron lee

d. Jamal Adams

343. Which two New York Jets players were tied with the most team sacks of 7 each for 2019?

a. Henry Anderson and Jordan Jenkins

b. Henry Anderson and Quinnen Williams

c. Jordan Jenkins and Quinnen Williams

d. Jamal Adams and Jordan Jenkins

344. In 2017 which 2 New York Jets players were tied with two interceptions each?

a. Buster Skrine and Darryl Roberts

b. Buster Skrine and Terrence Brooks

c. Terrence Brooks and Marcus Maye

d. Marcus Maye and Darryl Roberts

345. In 2015 which New York Jets player led the team in receiving yards?

a. Eric Decker

b. Quincy Enunwa

c. Jeremy Kerley

d. Brandon Marshall

346. In 2015 which New York Jets player led the team in sacks?

a. Leonard Williams

b. Muhammad Wilkerson

c. David Harris

d. Sheldon Richardson

347. In 2015 which New York jets player led the team in interceptions?

a. Marcus Williams

b. Darrelle Revis

c. Calvin Pryor

d. Marcus Gilchrist

348. Which New York Jets player had the most sacks in 2009?

a. David Harris

b. Shaun Ellis

c. Calvin Pace

d. Bryan Thomas

349. Which New York Jets player had the most interceptions in 2009?

a. Darrelle Revis

b. Kerry Rhodes

c. David Harris

d. Dwight Lowery

350. Which New York Jets player had the most solo tackles in 2009?

a. Bart Scott

b. Jim Leonhard

c. Kerry Rhodes

d. David Harris

351. In 2009 which New York Jets player had a 106 yard kickoff return?

a. Thomas Jones

b. Brad Smith

c. Shonn Greene

d. Leon Washington

352. Which New York Jets player had the most receiving yards in 2008?

a. Chansi Stuckey

b. Dustin Keller

c. Laveranues Coles

d. Jericho Cotchery

353. Which New York Jets player had a kickoff return average of 25.65 yards in 2008?

a. Leon Washington

b. Justin Miuller

c. Jericho Cotchery

d. Brad Smith

354. Which New York Jets player had the most solo tackles in 2008?

a. Abram Elam

b. Eric Barton

c. Kenyon Coleman

d. Shaun Ellis

355. Which New York Jets player had the most sacks in 2008?

a. Bryan Thomas

b. Kris Jenkins

c. Shaun Ellis

d. David Bowens

356. Which New York Jets player had the most interceptions in 2008?

a. Darrelle Revis

b. Kerry Rhodes

c. Dwight Lowery

d. Eric Smith

357. Which New York Jets player scored the most touchdowns in 2008?

a. Leon Washington

b. Lavernaeus Coles

c. Jericho Cotchery

d. Thomas Jones

358. Which New York Jets player had the most rushing yards in 2010?

a. Shonn Greene

b. Joe McKnight

c. LaDainian Tomlinson

d. Brad Smith

359. Which New York Jets player had the most sacks in 2010?

a. Calvin Pace

b. Bryan Thomas

c. .Jason Taylor

d. Drew Coleman

360. Which two New York Jets players were tied with 3 interceptions each in 2010?

a. Darrelle Revis and Antonio Cromarte

b. Dwight Lowery and Marquis Cole

c. Antonio Cromartie and Dwight Lowery

d. Jim Leonhard and Antonio Cromarte

361. Which New York Jets player had the most receiving touchdowns in 2010?

a. Braylon Edwards

b. Santonio Holmes

c. Dustin Keller

d. Jericho Cotchery

362. Which New York Jets player had the most interceptions in 2000?

a. Marcus Coleman

b. Aaron Glenn

c. Victor Green

d. Chris Hayes

363. Which New York Jets player had the most sacks in 2000?

a. Mo Lewis

b. Bryan Cox

c. Shaun Ellis

d. John Abraham

364. Which New York Jets player had the most fumble recoveries in 2000?

a. Mo Lewis

b. Bryan Cox

c. Victor Green

d. Shaun Ellis

365. Which New York Jets player had the most solo tackles in 2000?

a. Marvin Jones

b. Victor Green

c. Mo Lewis

d. Bryan Cox

366. Which New York Jets player had the most receiving yards in 2002?

a. Santana Moss

b. Laveranues Coles

c. Wayne Chrebet

d. Anthony Becht

367. Which New York Jets player had the most sacks in 2002?

a. Jason Ferguson

b. Josh Evans

c. Shaun Ellis

d. John Abraham

368. Which New York Jets player had the most receiving touchdowns in 2002?

a. Laveranues Coles

b. Anthony Becht

c. Wayne Chrebet

d. Santana Moss

369. Which New York Jets player had the most receiving yards in 1985?

a. Wesley Walker

b. Al Toon

c. Kurt Sohn

d. Mickey Shuler

370. Which New York Jets player had the most fumble recoveries in 1985?

a. Kyle Clifton

b. Mark Gastineau

c. Harry Hamilton

d. Kirk Springs

371. Which two New York Jets players were tied with four interceptions each in 1985 (the most interceptions by any player on the team for that year)?

a. Kerry Glenn and Bobby Jackson

b. Kerry Glenn and Lance Mehl

c. Bobby Jackson and Davlin Mullen

d. Bobby Jackson and Johnny Lynn

372. Which New York Jets player had the most receiving yards in 1993?

a. Chris Burkett

b. Terrance Mathis

c. Rob Moore

d. James Thornton

373. Which New York Jets player had the most receiving touchdowns in 1993?

a. Fred Baxter

b. Johnny Mitchell

c. James Thornton

d. Chris Burkett

374. Which New York Jets player had the most rushing touchdowns in 1993?

a. Blair Thomas

b. Johnny Johnson

c. Adrian Murrell

d. Brad Baxter

375. Which New York Jets player had the most interceptions in 1993?

a. Mo Lewis

b. Ronnie Lott

c. Brian Washington

d. James Hasty

376. Which New York Jets player had the most sacks in 1993?

a. Marvin Washington

b. Mo Lewis

c. Bobby Houston

d. Jeff Lageman

377. Which New York Jets player had the most receiving yards in 1998?

a. Keyshawn Johnson

b. Dedric Ward

c. Wayne Chrebet

d. Kyle Brady

378. Which New York Jets player had the most sacks in 1998?

a. Anthony Pleasant

b. Mo Lewis

c. Chad Cascadden

d. Bryan Cox

379. Which New York Jets player had the most solo tackles in 1998?

a. Mo Lewis

b. Victor Green

c. Otis Smith

d. Bryan Cox

380. Which New York Jets player caught the longest touchdown pass of 82 yards in 1998?

a. Dedric Ward

b. Wayne Chrebet

c. Leon Johnson

d. Keyshawn Johnson

381. Which New York Jets player had the most interceptions in 1998?

a. Victor Green

b. Aaron Glenn

c. Otis Smith

d. Ray Mickens

382. Which New York Jets player had the most rushing yards in 1991?

a. Blair Thomas

b. Brad Baxter

c. Freeman McNeil

d. Johnny Hector

383. Which New York Jets player had the most rushing touchdowns in 1991?

a. Johnny Hector

b. Brad Baxter

c. Freeman McNeil

d. Blair Thomas

384. Which New York Jets player had the most sacks in 1991?

a. Dennis Byrd

b. Marvin Washington

c. Jeff Lageman

d. Scott Mersereau

385. Which New York Jets player had the most solo tackles in 1991?

a. Kyle Clifton

b. Brian Washington

c. James Hasty

d. Mo Lewis

386. Which New York Jets player had an 84 yard interception return in 1991?

a. Lonnie Young

b. Michael Brim

c. James Hasty

d. Erik McMillan

387. Which New York Jets player had the most receiving touchdowns in 1991?

a. Al Toon

b. Terance Mathis

c. Rob Moore

d. Chris Burkett

388. Which New York Jets player had the most rushing touchdowns in 1981?

a. Kevin Long

b. Freeman McNeil

c. Mike Augustyniak

d. Bruce Harper

389. Which New York Jets player had the most receiving yards in 1981?

a. Johnny Lam Jones

b. Wesley Walker

c. Jerome Barkum

d. Derrick Gaffney

390. Which New York Jets player had the most interceptions in 1981?

a. Darrol Ray

b. Lance Mehl

c. Johnny Lynn

d. Greg Buttle

391. Which New York Jets player had two interception returns for touchdowns in 1981?

a. Jerry Holmes

b. Ken Schroy

c. Donald Dykes

d. Darrol Ray

392. Which New York Jets player had the most receiving yards in 2004?

a. Jerald Sowell

b. Santana Moss

c. Justin McCareins

d. Wayne Chrebet

393. Which New York Jets player had the most sacks in 2004?

a. John Abraham

b. Eric Barton

c. Shaun Ellis

d. Jason Ferguson

394. Which New York Jets player had the most solos tackles in 2004?

a. Eric Barton

b .Johnathan Vilma

c. Erik Coleman

d. David Barrett

395. Which New York Jets player had the most fumble recoveries in 2004?

a. Donnie Abraham

b. Eric Barton

c. Jason Glenn

d. Oliver Celestin

396. Which New York Jets player had the most receiving touchdowns in 1969?

a. George Sauer

b. Don Maynard

c. Bake Turner

d. Pete Lammons

397. Which New York Jets player had the most rushing yards in 1969?

a. Emerson Boozer

b. Bill Mathis

c. Matt Snell

d. Lee White

398. Which New York Jets player had the most receiving yards in 1969?

a. George Sauer

b. Pete Lammons

c. Bake Turner

d. Don Maynard

399. Matt Snell, Emerson Boozer and Bill Mathis all achieved the same feat in 1969?

a. They rushed for at least 600 yards each.

b. They each had four rushing touchdowns.

c. They each had 300 receiving yards.

d. They each fumbled three times.

400. Which New York Jets player caught a 57 yard touchdown pass from Joe Namath in 1969?

a. Don Maynard

b. George Sauer

c. Pete Lammons

d. Bake Turner

ANSWERS

341. C   342. B   343. A   344. C   345. D   346. B   347. A
348. C   349. A   350. D

351. B   352. D   353. A   354. B   355. C   356. A   357. D
358. C   359. B   360. C

361. A   362. C   363. A   364. C   365. A   366. B   367. D
368. C   369. D   370. B

371. A   372. C   373. B   374. D   375. C   376. D   377. A
378. B   379. B   380. C

381. B   382. A   383. B   384. C   385. A   386. D   387. C
388. D   389. B   390. A

391. D   392. B   393. C   394. A   395. B   396. A   397. C
398. D   399. B   400. A

CHAPTER XII:
NEW YORK JETS FUN FACTS

Bruce Harper was a running back and kick returner for the New York Jets from 1977-1984. In his career with the team, he had four consecutive 1,000 yard seasons. In those seasons, the yards were attained through rushing, receiving, kickoff and punt returns. Bruce holds the record as the all-time leader for the Jets in punt returns, punt return yardage, kickoff returns, and kickoff return yardage. In addition, in 1978 and 1980 he led the league by surpassing 2,000 all-purpose yards in each of those seasons.

Thomas Jones was a running back with the New York Jets from 2007 – 2009. In three years with the team, he rushed for 3,833 yards and scored 28 touchdowns. In 2008, he was selected to the Pro Bowl in a year in which he rushed for 1312 yards, scoring 13 rushing touchdowns. Thomas was also a valuable receiver and caught 74 passes for 282 yards. His total offensive output for the team all-time was 4,315 yards and 31 touchdowns on 1,005 touches. He certainly was a great acquisition for the team and achieved a great amount of production in a short period of time.

Ken O'Brien was the New York Jets quarterback from 1983–1992. He was selected to two Pro Bowls, and in 1985 led the NFL in passing with a 96.2 passer rating. He holds the record for the most completions in team history with 2,039. Ken threw for 25,094 yards in his career with the team along with 28 touchdowns against 98 interceptions.

Darrelle Revis was a cornerback with the New York Jets from 2007– 2012. He was a first round selection in 2007 and was selected to four Pro Bowls with the team. He was a great shut down corner and defended 16 passes in his rookie year and 31 passes in 2009. He was nicknamed "Revis Island" and had the reputation that no wide receiver could overtake him. He did not play in a Super Bowl with the Jets but achieved a Super Bowl ring with the rival Patriots. The only dark side of his career was the continual contractual issues he had with the team involving several holdouts. Overall, he was a great defensive player for the team.

Pat Leahy was a placekicker with the New York Jets from 1974-1991. He was a very consistent placekicker with the team kicking 304 field goals with 558 point after attempts.

In addition, he successfully kicked 22 of 30 field goal attempts and is the Jets leading scorer in team history with 1470 points.

John Abraham was acquired through free agency in 2000 and played for the New York Jets from 2000-2005. He was a defensive end with the team and averaged almost 9 sacks per season. John was selected to three Pro Bowls and achieved 19 forced fumbles during his tenure with the team. After leaving the team, John had four double digit sack years with other teams. If John would have spent his entire career with the franchise, he likely would have been the team's all-time sack leader.

Mo Lewis was a linebacker with the New York Jets from 1991-2003. He is the team's all-time leader in tackles with 1,231. Mo was selected to three consecutive Pro Bowls and had 14 interceptions with the team. In addition, he had 52.5 sacks, recovered 18 opponent's fumbles, and had 29 forced fumbles in his career with the team.

Shaun Ellis was a Defensive End with the New York Jets from 2000-2010. He holds the team record for playing in 170 games on the defensive line. He is third in team history with 72.5 sacks, and recorded multiple sacks in three or more consecutive games. In addition, he was selected to two Pro Bowls and recorded 13 forced fumbles with the team.

Freeman McNeil was a running back with the New York Jets from 1981-1992. In twelve seasons and 144 games with the team, he rushed for 8,074 yards, second in team history. In addition, he had 2,961 receiving yards, second in team history to Curtis Martin. Freeman was selected to three Pro Bowls and played in more games than any other New York Jets running back.

Wesley Walker was a wide receiver with the New York Jets from 1977-1989. In his career with the team, he amassed 8,306 receiving yards, second in team history to Don Maynard. In 1978, Wesley led the NFL in receiving with 1,169 yards and averaged 24.4 yards per catch. He was selected to two Pro Bowls, and his career record of 19 yards per catch, and 24.4 yards per catch in 1978, are still team records.

Joe Namath was the fourth starting quarterback for the New York Jets. He was the first quarterback to throw for over 4,000 yards in a season. The 4,000 yard record he held was broken in 1979 by Dan Fouts. Joe was AFL Rookie of the Year in 1965 and also was a two time AFL MVP. In addition, Joe's career passing yards, touchdown passes, and passing attempts to this day are still team records. Joe led his team to win Super Bowl III despite the fact that he did not throw a touchdown pass in the game. In his career, Joe threw 170 touchdown passes against 215 interceptions. Overall, Joe's cumulative record with the New York Jets is 60 wins, 61 losses and 4 ties.

Don Maynard was a wide receiver with the New York Jets from 1960-1972. He played one year for the New York Giants and joined the Jets when they were the New York Titans. In 13 years with the Jets, Don had five 1,000 receiving yard seasons and a career total of 11,732 receiving yards. Don's career receiving yards and 633 career receptions are still a team record today.

CONCLUSION

Each football season presents the opportunity for every NFL team to improve their roster. The New York Jets were very active in free agency in 2021 and addressed several positions of need. In addition, Joe Douglas also bolstered positions of need throughout the draft. Time will only tell if the selections he made will develop into the playmakers the team desperately needs. It will also be interesting to see if any of the Undrafted Free Agents he chose will make the team. I also will be paying close attention to the rookies selected in the draft to see if they will break records set by the rookies who preceded them.

Prior to the draft, the New York Jets set out to find a replacement for Sam Darnold. In selecting Zach Wilson with the first pick of the draft, they possibly have found their franchise quarterback. The team also needs to find a backup to Zach Wilson; the two other quarterbacks on the team have not thrown a pass in an NFL regular season game. In addition, their backup quarterback of 2020, Joe Flacco, signed with the Philadelphia Eagles.

In 2020, the New York Jets lacked a true number one and number two receiver. Fortunately, Joe Douglas addressed the wide receiver position in free agency with the signings of Corey Davis and Keelan Cole. In addition, Joe addressed the receiver positional need in the draft. Overall, it appears on paper that the New York Jets have a much stronger receiver unit than they had in 2020.

One major surprise of the 2021 draft is that Joe Douglas waited until the fifth round to address the cornerback position. The weakest part of the team in 2021 was their secondary. Joe selected a few players for the secondary in the fifth and sixth rounds. Time will only tell if the cornerbacks and safeties he selected will eventually become effective starters for the team.

The 2021 season will be upon us shortly and another year of stats will be recorded. In addition, records will be broken and this information will be recorded and be a part of future trivia books. Sports trivia is and always will be a great conversational piece at parties and certainly will test the wit of those who engage in it. I really enjoyed creating this book as I had the opportunity to write about my favorite sports team. Bye for now, but I will be seeing you soon with the release of yet another book!

Tyler Crawford

Printed in Dunstable, United Kingdom